SPRING
New Life Everywhere

by Janet McDonnell
illustrated by Linda Hohag

created by Wing Park Publishers

CHILDRENS PRESS®

CHICAGO

Library of Congress Cataloging-in-Publication Data

McDonnell, Janet, 1962-
   Spring : new life everywhere / by Janet McDonnell ;
illustrated by Linda Hohag.
      p.   cm. — (The Four Seasons)
   "Created by Wing Park Publishers."
   Summary: Trying to find the owner of an egg he has found
in the spring, Mouse calls on many animals and finds new
life everywhere he goes.
  ISBN 0-516-00677-0
   [1. Spring—Fiction. 2. Eggs—Fiction. 3. Mice—Fiction.
4. Animals—Fiction.] I. Hohag, Linda, ill. II. Title. III.
Series.
PZ7.M478436Sp 1993
[E]—dc20   93-10309
                                   CIP
                                   AC

SPRING
New Life Everywhere

ne bright morning, Mouse came out of his burrow and found a surprise. The snow had all melted! "At last!" he cried. "Spring is really here!"

All around him, the forest seemed to be waking up after a long sleep. Two squirrels

chased each other up and down a tree. A
butterfly flew past Mouse's nose. White and
purple flowers poked up from the ground,
and the branches of the trees were filled with
fat buds.

Best of all, there was plenty of food to be found. Mouse scurried about, nibbling on seeds and tender green leaves. As he ate, he heard a bird singing. Mouse looked up. "Robin!" he cried. "I haven't seen you for a long time. Where have you been?"

"We flew south for the winter. But now we're back," said Robin. "I have a surprise. Come, take a look."

Mouse climbed up to peek into Robin's
nest. He saw three skinny little birds, all
cheeping at the same time. Their beaks were
wide open. "Wow, they sure look hungry!"
said Mouse.

"They are," said Robin.

Mouse noticed one blue egg in the bottom of the nest. "What's wrong with this one?" he asked.

"Oh, there must be a slowpoke in that egg," said Robin. "He'll come out soon. I'd better get food for the others!"

"That reminds me, I'm still hungry," said Mouse. And off he went to finish his breakfast.

As Mouse scampered about looking for buds, he saw something strange. It was under a bush. He went to take a closer look. "It's an egg!" said Mouse. "But I've never seen an egg like this. Maybe Robin will know who this belongs to," he said.

He picked up the egg and ran back to see Robin.

"Hmm, this sure is a strange egg," said Robin. "Maybe it belongs to Chipmunk. I've heard that she is about to become a mother. I've never seen a chipmunk's eggs before, but maybe they look like this!"

"Thanks, Robin," said Mouse. And off he ran.

Mouse pushed the egg down the hole of
Chipmunk's burrow and ran in after it, calling,
"Chipmunk, Chipmunk, I've found your egg."
"My egg?" said Chipmunk. "Don't be silly.
Chipmunks don't lay eggs."

"But Robin said you were about to become a mother," said Mouse.

"I am a mother. But my babies didn't hatch from eggs," said Chipmunk. "Here they are." She showed Mouse four furry little babies asleep in a soft nest.

"But if this isn't your egg, then whose is it?" asked Mouse.

"Try Duck. I've heard that she has a nest full of eggs. Maybe she lost one," said Chipmunk.

"Good idea," said Mouse.

Mouse ran all the way to the pond, being careful not to drop the egg. He found Duck's nest hidden behind some cattails. But the nest was empty! Just then, Mouse saw Duck in the tall grass by the edge of the pond.

"Duck, Duck, I've found your egg!" cried Mouse.

"Why, I'm not missing an egg," said Duck, and she jumped into the pond with a splash. There were five more splashes as five yellow ducklings jumped into the pond after her. "I had five eggs, but they all hatched," said Duck. "Now I have five ducklings. This is their first swimming lesson."

"Do you know anyone else who lays eggs?"
asked Mouse.

"Certainly," said Duck. "Frog lays eggs."

Mouse looked all around until he found
Frog sunning herself on a rock. "Frog, Frog,
I've found your egg!" cried Mouse.

When Frog saw the egg, she laughed and laughed. "That's not my egg," she said. "My eggs are tiny and see-through, with black dots in the middle. I lay them in the water. And besides, my eggs have all hatched."

"Where are your babies?" asked Mouse.

"Over here. Take a look," said Duck.

Mouse leaned over the water's edge and saw a group of squirmy tadpoles.

"But they don't look like you," said Mouse.

"They will," said Frog. "They will lose their tails and grow legs so they can hop like I do."

"It seems there are new babies every-where," said Mouse. "Baby robins, baby chipmunks, baby ducks, and now baby frogs. I wish I knew what kind of baby is in this egg. One thing is for sure. I have to find its mama before it hatches. But how?"

"Why don't you ask Ground Hog?" said
Frog. "He knows all the animals of the forest."
"Good idea!" said Mouse. And he was off.

By the time Mouse reached Ground Hog,
he was out of breath. "Ground Hog, I'm so
glad to see you," he said. "I need your help
to find out who this egg belongs to."

Ground Hog chuckled. "I don't think you
need to worry, Mouse," he said. "Someone
will come looking for that egg pretty soon."
"What do you mean?" asked Mouse.

Just then, they heard the pounding of running feet. A little boy was heading their way! Mouse was so scared, he forgot the egg. Then he and Ground Hog ran to hide.

"I found one!" cried the boy. He bent down and picked up the egg. Mouse almost ran after the boy, but Ground Hog stopped him.

"Let me go! I have to save that egg!" cried Mouse.

"Don't worry, there's no baby in that egg," said Ground Hog. "I saw one crack open once. That's what I was about to tell you. This happens every spring. A big person comes and hides a bunch of strange looking eggs. Then children come to find the eggs. It sounds like a silly game to me."

Mouse was sad. "I was kind of excited about seeing that egg hatch," he said.

Just then, he heard Robin calling, "Mouse! Mouse! It's happening! Come see!"

Mouse and Ground Hog ran as fast as they could to Robin's nest.

"Our slowpoke is finally coming out to say hello to spring," said Robin.

Mouse leaned down to get a closer look. His whiskers twitched with excitement. Suddenly, there was a *Crrack*, and another *Crrack!* Out popped a little yellow beak. It

startled Mouse so he nearly fell out of the tree.

Ground Hog laughed. "You see, Mouse? You got to see an egg hatch after all. That's what spring is all about—the beginning of new life!"

Mouse looked closely at the little bird in the eggshell. "Hello, Spring!" he said.

You have read what Mouse does in the Spring.
Here are some things children do.

Can you read the words?

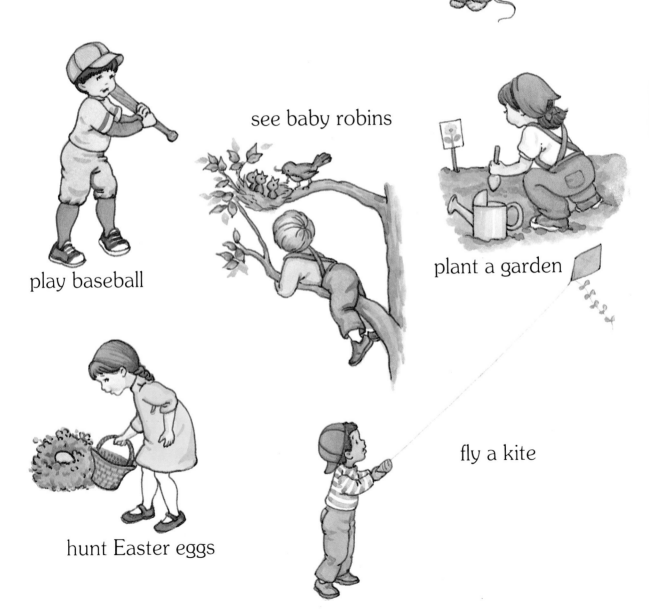

see baby robins

play baseball

plant a garden

hunt Easter eggs

fly a kite

Can you think of other things?